BMX
Action Bike Book

No BMX bike is unbreakable. The stunts and techniques in this book owe as much to the skill of the riders as they do to the strength of the bikes. Anybody can break a bike. It takes ability to take it to the limits and keep yourself and your bike in one piece.

If you are about to attempt a trick that means landing your bike like a ten ton tank, then think again. You are probably doing it wrong.

Remember land light, ALWAYS wear safety gear and work out away from traffic.

Happy landings.

Purnell

Words	Richard Grant and Nigel Thomas Editors BMX Action Bike Magazine
Photography	Richard "The Crouch" Francis
Additional Photography	"The Cap"
Photo Research	James "Okie Dokie" Black
Layout	Nigel "Marvellous" Standerline Pete "Two Shirts" Williams
Typeset	Project Reprographics, Chichester

Freestyle aerial on page 29 demonstrated by Bob Haro is published by kind permission of Bob Haro and is taken from his manual of trick riding, "Freestyle Moves".

Designed and produced by Autumn Publishing Ltd, 10 Eastgate Square, Chichester, Sussex and BMX Action Bike Magazine, 134 Tooley Street, London SEI.

This edition published by Purnell Books, Paulton, Bristol BS18 5LQ

ISBN 0361 06323 7

Printed by CGP Delo, Yugoslavia

The Editors would like to thank in no particular order the following who managed to bribe their way into this book: Steve Clark, Mark 'Sid' Salisbury, Mad Malc Stapleton, Bob Haro, Andy Ruffell, Chris Young, Glen Holderness, Timmy Judge, Rich Farside Nelson Chanady, Bob Medrano, Andy Patterson, Tony Butty, Edouard Gardier, Alan Woods, Clint Miller, Billy Stupple, Keith Wilson, Greg Alderman, Ian Ruby, Addie van der Ven, Tony Slater, Greg Hill, Stu Thomsen, Harry Leary, Neil Stevens, Wayne Llewellyn, Tim March, Scott Williams, Gary 'Morocco' Fenwick, Harvey Munkton, Ian Harrison, Darren and Jolyon Stock, Conrad Buffong, Dave Sanderson, Junkyard Jim Martin and everyone who's name we left out, including whatshisname.

UK location photography at: Harrow skatepark, the No-Name track Rad City, various Streets of London, Birmingham Wheels, Nottingham, Halfords Redditch Anglo-American, Halfords Birmingham NEC, Lee Cooper Picketts Lock, Bradford Bandits, Magna Mustangs Wimborne plus the Dartford chalk pits. Overseas location photography at: USA: Knotts Berry Farm, Ca, Haro's old LA factory, Las Vegas Jag Worlds and Kendall, Fla. Europe: Slagharen IBMXF Worlds, Holland; European Championships Beek & Donk, Holland; European Championships Palais De Congres Dijon, France.

Our thanks also for Staff support services (nosh) to the "O' Sole Mio" cafe, Tooley Street, London.

Contents

HEALTH WARNING. BMX fever is catching. It can completely alter your way of life. Those unaffected should put down this book at once. Otherwise the authors will not be held responsible for the consequences.

BMX Fever

The first known symptoms of BMX fever were diagnosed in Southern California in 1969.

The early victims were all young and addicted to racing street Choppers across dirt tracks. When they fell apart, the bikes were modified with parts cannibalised from machines beyond repair. Early experiments in frame and fork design happened late at night with borrowed welding equipment in home workshops.

In an effort to contain outbreaks of the fever an enterprising race promoter invited riders to race on his motorbike motocross track. This was a mistake. Bicycle motocross, as BMX was then known, took off. Purpose-built tracks sprung up all over California. Rapidly the disease spread like wildfire across America, crossed oceans, swept continents and is now a worldwide epidemic. Wherever it is encountered the spread of the symptoms is the same. Victims go to any lengths to obtain BMX machines. All it takes is the discovery that these 20 inch wheel, rugged, single-gear bikes are twice as versatile as anything else calling itself a bicycle. The realisation that the bike can be raced, stunted and jumped is enough. Quickly they progress to the next stage of the disease, exhibiting strong desires to 'get rad'.

Tell-tale signs include long hours on the bike, practising small bunnyhop jumps, building makeshift ramps to get air and learning to swing the bike full circle. They mutter words such as moto, berm, rad, gnarly in everyday conversation. At this point, the case is hopeless. There is no known cure. Only more BMX.

Once enough BMX riders group together, the community is in danger. A BMX track is demanded. Powerful forces, parents, friends, bike shops and youth workers come to their aid. The argument that BMX is just another passing two year craze like skateboards is quickly defeated. BMX has lasted longer. Bikes are a natural form of travel and tracks are cheaper to build than skateparks. They can be built in days, require no special construction and no more land than a soccer pitch. One track quickly leads to another. Clubs and teams form. Riders get sponsored to ride at local, regional and national level. They race indoors and outdoors for trophies to treasure, points for No 1 plates and, sometimes, for money. They don't mind scratches, bruises, blistered hands, or worn-out jeans. Their machinery is always the best and in need of improvement. Whether freestyle or racer, they are always on the lookout for new equipment to make the bikes lighter, slicker and quicker.

More and more earn their living from their demonstrating and just plain racing BMX.

At the top of their sport they are interviewed on TV and radio, photographed by the papers, travel the world to race and are treated as heroes by people their own age.

Their future predictions for BMX include bigger, better, longer tracks, more prize money, more TV coverage and stronger, lighter machinery.

No-one knows where it will end. Only one thing is sure. BMX fever is here. To stay!

Outdoor Racing

The tracks are the theatres of BMX. Yet you find them in the oddest places. Down muddy farm lanes, beneath inner city motorway intersections, inside greyhound stadiums and on windy moorland tops. Stumble across one on a non-race day and mistake it for a deserted road construction site. Come back on race day and it's alive. Hundreds of riders in bright coloured team gear, rows of upturned, shiny, chrome-moly machinery in the paddock, ultra sharp team buses, families, support crews, mobile bike shops, food sellers. Bustle and excitement as the motosheets are posted, chat, gossip, your name announced over the loudspeakers, the muffled roar of the crowd heard from inside a helmet. The scene.

Above: Changing the angle and direction of the bike in mid-air is one skill. Doing it under the intense gaze of a crowd supporting the other guy, is another! Dutchman Leon Walravens has both, and this explains why he is respected throughout Europe.

Race organisation can be as slick as the actual racing. At first-class meets, wave after wave of riders will thunder out of the gate at the rate of a moto a minute. It is the only way 600 riders can race three times in an afternoon and progress through to finals. From the start, riders line up for their moto action according to age group. In the qualifying motos the same eight race each other three times. Only their gate positions change from moto to moto. The overall first four qualify for the next round of quarter finals, then semis. These are sudden death. The first four across the line qualify for the main event where the action reaches its climax. It's the winners of the mains who take home trophies and earn points that count towards that all-important No 1 plate.

Dusty tracks throw up their own tactics, like this dustcloud for obscuring the rest of the pack's vision.

Above: Races can be won or lost over the first speedjump. The art is to keep the bike low and the back wheel glued for traction.

Outdoor Racing

Before any big race, top riders prepare their bikes and their bodies. Then on race day they fine-tune their minds. Pre-race, they slowly pace the track, calculating the best gearing to use and the tyres for the best traction. The lines to protect when in front are noted and where to strike from the pack. In the early motos they linger by the start hill for the rhythm of the starter's chant — "Riders Ready, Pedals Ready.. Go!" They dance through the start motion minus bikes, trying to pick up the beat. It looks weird but it pays! They're usually the riders out of the gate first.

You take the high line and I'll take the low line..... and I get stuck at the back of the pack. On cereal bowl berms, like the one above, the shortest inside line is not always the quickest. Better to ride the berm and take the natural advantage of cemtrifugal force.

BMX racing knows no age limits. As soon as you can balance on a bike and pedal, you are in business. The youngest recorded racers are 4 years old, although officially they race as under 6s.

Track Focus

The fastest, strongest, best-equipped riders still need trackcraft. It's a combo of bike skills plus tactical sense. Before a race, riders pace round a track, examining obstacles, calculating the fastest line, deciding where to overtake and where to be wary of sudden challenges.

The start is still the most important part of the race. Before their moto, shrewd racers hang around the gate listening to the starter's timing — "Riders Ready, Pedals Ready, Go!" Memorising the speed of his voice and the exact moment when the gate drops pays off. It sharpens reflexes that can lead to a splitsecond advantage and give the fastest possible start.

Below: These Australian-style step-up jumps have a wicked twist. Just when you want to keep the bike low they throw you into the air — as second place realises too late.

Below: Flying high has crowd appeal but little else going for it. Too much time in the air is too little time on the ground. The rider nearest camera has the right idea, taking it fast and low. His mid-air quarter turn is also the smart move on this track, setting the bike up for the coming lefthand sweeper turn.

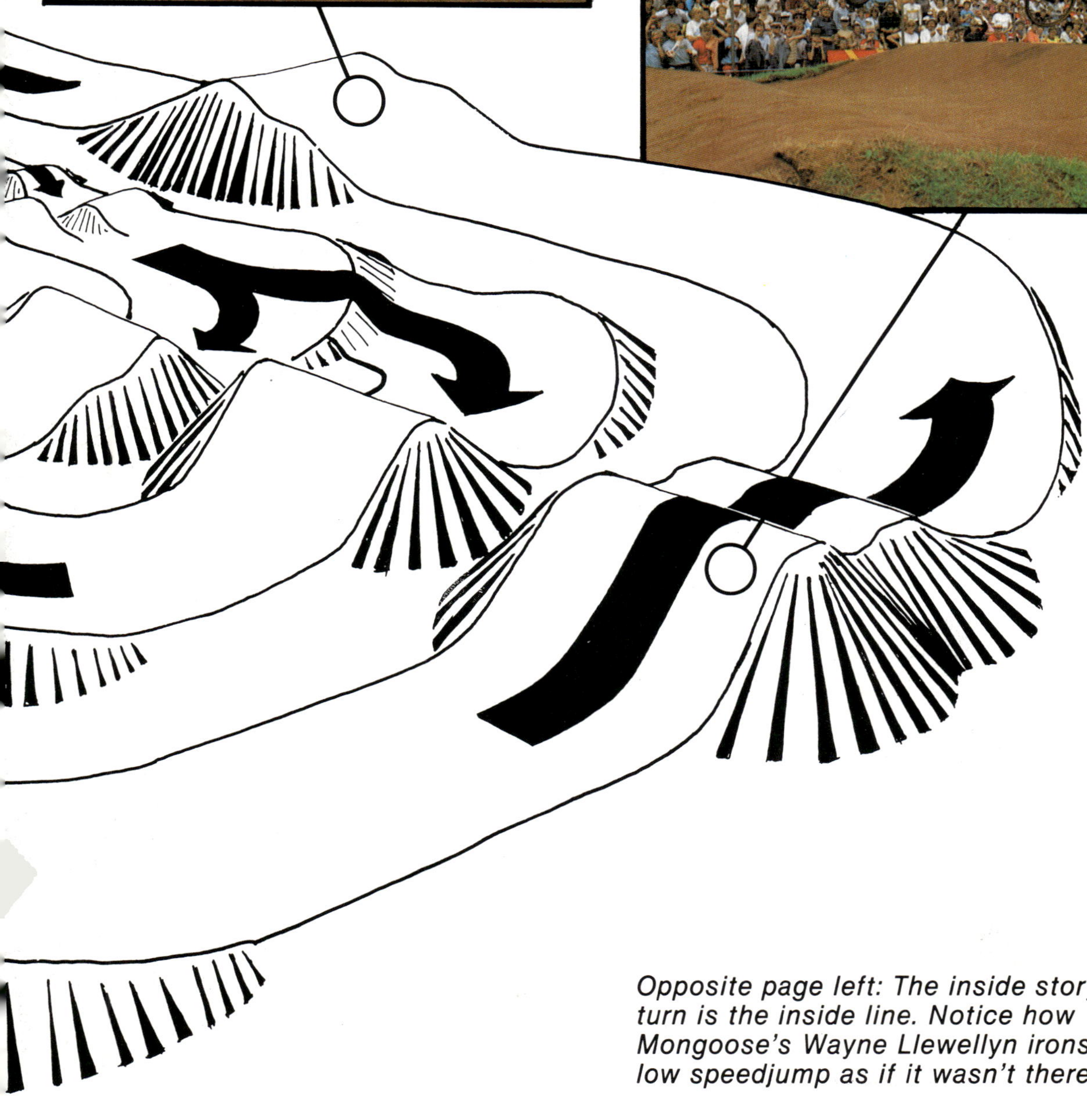

Opposite page left: The inside story on this turn is the inside line. Notice how Mongoose's Wayne Llewellyn irons out the low speedjump as if it wasn't there.

Track Focus

No matter how many times you cruise round a track there's no substitute for racing with seven other riders at your elbow, all jostling for the lead. A moto actually only lasts 30 seconds. But after, it feels like a lifetime. Win or lose you live and re-live every hard-fought inch, every runaway second. Finding out what-went-wrong-and-where is part of improving in BMX. Tactics are half the race. Learning how to handle them in the fury of a moto is the other half, as some of these riders are demonstrating.

Top right: Tim March has got the lead on the berm. And he's not giving it away. The left foot hanging over, effectively blocks the line for the rider behind.

Below: Traction is action. If the back wheel isn't glued to the dirt over jumps, then speed drops. And at this point in the moto it could be curtains to a trophy.

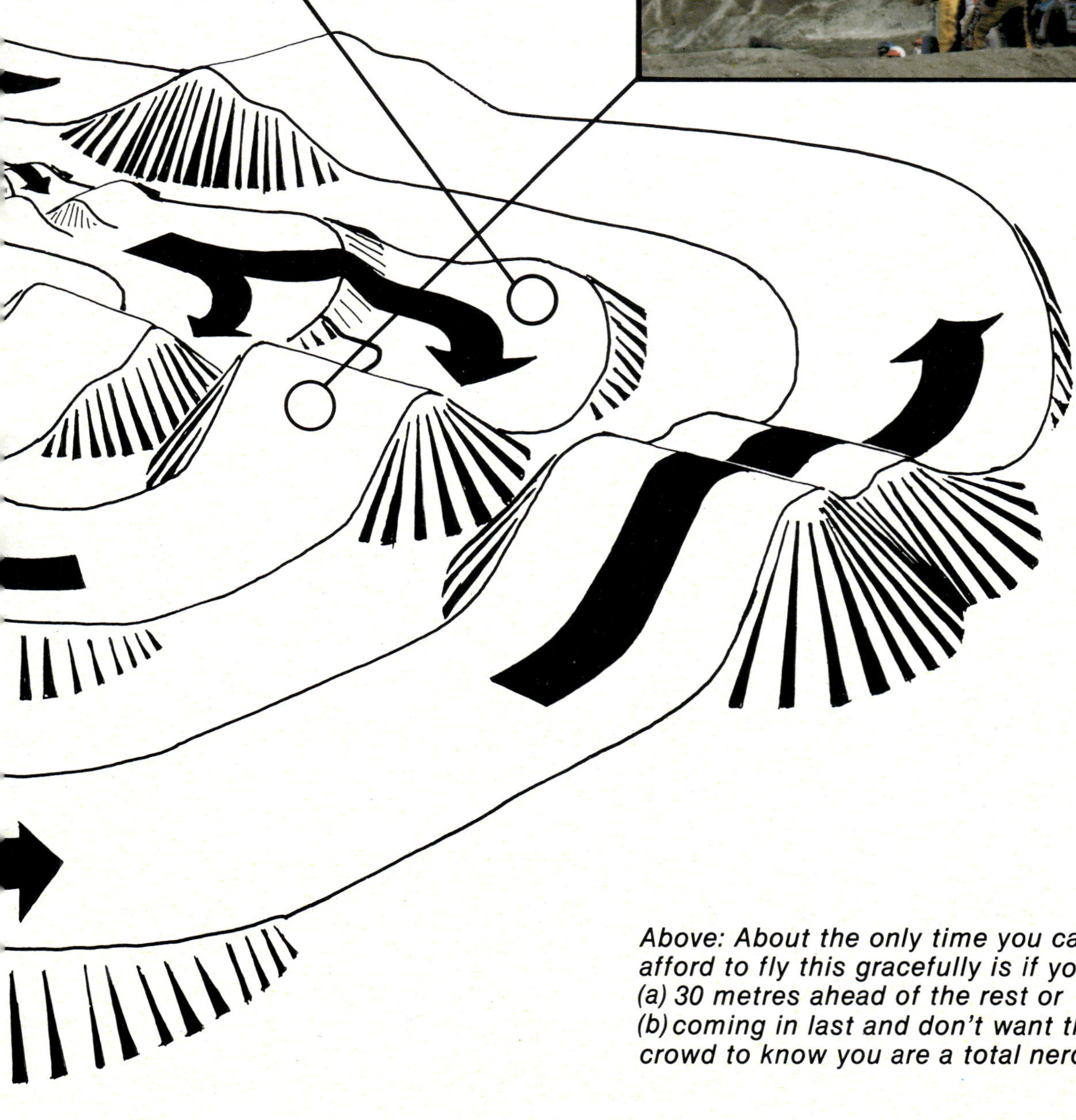

Above: About the only time you can afford to fly this gracefully is if you're (a) 30 metres ahead of the rest or (b) coming in last and don't want the crowd to know you are a total nerd.

Heroes in Helmets

These are the famous. The riders who've made it to the top in BMX by winning. They are interviewed on TV and radio. They get their pictures in the colour magazines. At the tracks they sign autographs for fans of their own age. They star in TV commercials, write articles, teach BMX at demos and can make their living from the sport. Some stay as amateurs but the best in America turn professional. They ride for money and can come away from a two-day race richer by £10,000 for just a few minutes racing, thanks to prize money and bonus payments from sponsors. But to reach that peak they will have put in long hours of training, exercise and practice.

Apart from twice winning the European Superclass, US pro rider, Andy Patterson, (above) has a useful sideline. He invents and sells BMX products which are aimed at making little bikes bigger for larger riders like himself. The laidback seatpost and pedal extenders were among his gifts to the outsize BMX-kind.

Like many BMX stars, Dutch and European open champion, Addie van der Ven, (left) used to ride motorbike motocross. Now he prefers BMX. Could it be because it has given him a full-time job and made Addie a national hero?

Left: The UK's first homegrown hero, Andy Ruffell, is a rare combination of top racer and ace freestyler. On the track he has twice won his age group No 1 plate, as well as winning most of the major UK freestyle contests. Friendly and easy-going, he's made scores of TV and radio appearances in the UK and overseas.

Below: Alice Temple isn't too keen on the limelight but cannot help getting it since she became the first girl to grab the girls' No 1 plate two years in a row. Whenever she can, Alice races against boys to raise her skill level. She also hopes to start her own BMX company.

Heroes in Helmets

Harry Leary (left) is one of the trailblazers of pro racing. Of the original eight to line-up for the first pro money race, Harry has gone on to be one of the sports high earners. He receives a salary from Diamond Back and six co-sponsors. Known as Scary Leary for his aggressive riding style, he rides best when under pressure. Off track, he is keen on developing new BMX prototypes and was the first pro rider to design and autograph a production line BMX machine.

When he's not dropping his ultra low gear bike off the tops of cars, or hopping pallet stacks, Oscar Bujadon scoots down sheersided, rockstrewn mountain paths. One of the clown princes of Spanish BMX. He needs a helmet!

Between them, top US professional riders, Greg Hill (above left) and Stu Thomsen, are BMX's all-time top prize money earners. Stu has twice been top money. Greg, who went pro at 14, has been top three times. Greg also won the first three pro World Championship titles, and came second the fourth time round.
Nicknamed the Mohammed Ali of BMX, 19 year old Greg strains his mind as much as his body to win. Stu, nearly 25, is the oldest of the original pros and is frequently asked how much longer he can go on. Replies: "Until I stop winning".

One of Britain's most popular riders, Tim March (left) has twice won UK No 1 plates and taken two European titles. Runs ace coaching sessions, designs and makes his own numberplates.

Picture Dictionary

THE TABLETOP. Part of any self-respecting freestyler's inventory of tricks. So called because the bike is laid so flat that you could serve lunch on it (if it wasn't flying through the air!). Experts rate the manoeuvre according to degrees of flatness achieved. Perfect is plain 'flat'. In degrees of radness 'overflat' will leave the crowd gawping but the purists complaining. Skill level required—better than competent, more than fearless but not quite insane! By the time you attempt this, bunnyhopping must be elementary, getting air a daily habit.

NB The aerial tabletop is not to be confused with the obstacle of the same name found on most tracks.

THE WHEELIE. (right) Simply the art of travelling on one wheel. Usually performed with the rear wheel driving and the front suspended in the air. (A few awkward customers are now developing the front wheel wheelie.) The rear wheel wheelie is used in BMX racing to help set the bike up for speedjumps (see opposite).
There are also wheelie specialists who do nothing but challenge one another to establish non-stop world records. The first one was just over 42 minutes. The latest record is close to four hours. Skill needed—competent bike handling and patience. Practise in private. Expect to slip off the back before you get the hang of it.

THE SPEEDJUMP. (above) Once mastered will turn mountains into molehills. Is an absolutely standard and easy to learn technique. Essential for BMX racing. The basic principle is to keep your wheels glued to the ground as much as possible. Getting bags of air may look exciting but during a race speed is essential. A rider flying through the ozone is on average 5 mph slower than one burning rubber on the dirt. The art of the speedjump is to pedal all the way through the jump. Standard technique is to pre-wheelie, lifting the front wheel just a few pedals before the jump. As the front wheel clears the brow it drops down. Shift your weight back over the rear wheel and pedal away.

Picture Dictionary

RAD. Abbreviation of radical. Means insane, fearless, off-the-wall, plain crazy, beyond nuts. Totally rad riders believe in getting ultra-gnarly and going flat-out critical. Stunts and speed are their style. Eating, sleeping, riding, talking, breathing, dreaming, living and loving BMX is their way of life.
If you've got one trick or track wired and want to move on to the next. If every new mound of dirt or road construction site is examined eagle-eyed for jump possibilities. If you constantly invent new and unbelievable ways to trick out your bike. Then you're beginning to think rad!

Right: Master of radness, Chris Young. Some characters are happy just to get up there. Guys like Chris make sure they get rad up there squeezing maximum hang time out of every jump. That way they can freeze longer in the air and execute delicate little turndowns like this, just in case there's a photographer around in search of a rad picture.

BERM. (top of opposite page) A banked bend. Term originally borrowed from motorbike motocross. No self-respecting BMX track will have less than three of these. Properly designed, a berm lets the rider sweep round a curve without dropping speed or wiping out. Berms come in all shapes and sizes. Saucer and cereal bowls are the most common design. The first berm is often the most critical point in the race. Whoever holds the lead will go for the midway line where speed is highest but leaves no room for anyone to pass beneath. Second place tactics are to run outside and try to turn sharply to cut inside the lead rider. Sometimes known as berm warfare!

BUNNYHOP. (right) Basic BMX manoeuvre for avoiding obstacles. Once mastered, allows the rider to jump clean over tree stumps, rocks, ditches, etc. Requires no ramp. Can be performed stationary with pedals level. However, attempts like Andy Ruffell's on the world record (42 inches, 106.6 cms) require run-ups for momentum before lift-off. Getting air like this requires practice, skill, energy, nerve and legs like springs. The thrill of clearing the bar achieves the same satisfaction as the novice gets from making a bike jump a millimetre off the ground.

Picture Dictionary

THE HOLESHOT. (below) This is often taken to mean the rider who gets out the gate first. Others believe it refers to the racer who crosses the first obstacle first. And others, mainly of the California school, believe it refers to the person leading at the first turn. Actually, not worth arguing about! Far better to make sure you get it, whatever it is?

THE AERIAL. (right) Sometimes known as 'getting air' for obvious reasons. Demonstrated here by Mr William Stupple of Skyway. Requires a fast run-up, plus a ramp with some vert (see quarterpipe entry on this page). Also bags of nerve. Much more fun to do than write or read about. Safety gear 100% essential.

THE QUARTERPIPE. (inset, right) So called because it is the shape of one quarter of a pipe (get it, dummy?). Essential equipment for serious freestyler. Construction can be all wood, or mix of metal frame and wood deck. Early models in high density, clear perspex looked good but proved defective. Vert (meaning vertical) area at the top of the quarterpipe helps in getting air. Always wear safety gear and make sure the quarterpipe is firmly braced.

RECREATION

Freestyle

Freestyle is the art of total bike control. The art of making the bike and you do what you want, where you want and exactly when you want. It's a tall order! The top practitioners are constantly stretching the dimensions of what is possible beyond previously imagined limits. Long hours of practice are put in, inventing and perfecting new moves, new tricks for roller smooth shows where their bikes do everything but sing. They are as agile as gymnasts, as graceful as ice skaters and as daring as stuntmen. Some use special freestyle bikes, others regular BMX frames. They run harder tyre pressures than racers, nylon wheels and often a third coaster back-pedal brake. And they ALWAYS wear safety gear—a helmet, pair of gloves, long pants and long sleeve jerseys or elbow protectors.

The copyright on this mid-air manoeuvre, with the front wheel dipped and the back end rising, belongs to a Mr Trashcan Morgan. Perfectly executed here for our cameras by twice European champion, Andy Patterson.

Below: Kickturns on quarterpipes require good balance and a cool head. At the top of the ramp the weight is over the back and the bars put the front wheel ready for re-entry.

At the bottom of the page we see that some people can't do anything the right way round! Climbing on from the front, using the bars as a saddle and pedalling backwards, just sort of appeals to groundtricks specialist Neil Stevens.

Freestyle

Freestyle riding is just like learning to ride a bike. Once you've got a trick wired, you never lose the knack. But acquiring that mastery requires practice. Concentrate on learning one trick at a time, just like the top freestylers. Like this character (below) making a meal out of a no-kerb-endo, keep running the trick over and over again. Then you become more consistent and knock off the rough edges. Once it's down to a fine art you can begin to push the limits (you can even find a kerb). Having a friend around helps. You have someone to advise you on what looks right and where you might be going wrong. Other times, music helps your concentration. Always remember that learning tricks is a process of trial and error. Be prepared for things to go wrong from time to time. Especially aerial tricks. Protective clothing helps but if you've got to bail out, and the choice is between you and the bike crashing, make sure it's the bike. It can take it!

Why is this a 'hip hanger'?
—'cos his hip is hanging out, dummy!

There is air and there is air. Getting it is Bob Haro, the guru of freestyle, numberplate tycoon and some time stunt star of ET. Clearing this much height requires no little talent, plenty of nerve, bags of experience and, er, um... confidence in the people holding the quarterpipe.

Freestyle Tricks

THE BAR HOP.
Choose a quiet spot away from traffic. Dry-run minus the bike using a chair without arms, set up 2½ metres from a table. Pull your knees up to your chin and swing them out towards the table. On the bike:
Start from sitting and coast along medium to fast. The last turn of the pedals should leave them level.
Shift your weight up to pivot on your wrists. Tuck your legs up so your knees are under your chin.
Swing your legs forward to just hop clear of the bars. Legs straight, sit on bars.
Dismount by hopping off the front or reversing procedure. Wear safety gear!

Quarterpipe aerials are the flash side of freestyle. But beware. Says freestyle maestro Bob Haro, "The thing most riders do wrong is to loop the bike out and land on the bottom of the ramp." Instead, touchdown on the point you took off from. If Bob makes it look easy, it isn't. Aerials take time and practice.

Hearts of Steel

Welcome to the machines. Topline BMX bikes didn't just happen. They evolved from the Choppers, Grifters and Stingrays of the past. Today, creating a production BMX bike requires months of exhaustive design, research and development. Every angle of frame geometry is calculated for performance.

❶ Shotgun saddle. Earns its nickname because the aerodynamic seat is shot full of weight-saving holes. Construction is solid not soft. In BMX races there's seldom time to sit down. Instead riders raise their saddles high to stabilise the bike in tight corners.

❷ Seatclamp. Hinged for easy adjustment, manufactured from tough chrome-moly, secured by one bolt and designed not to rattle loose.

❸ Alloy wheels are the lightest of all. Nylon mag wheels are heavier but absorb impact and last longer.

❹ Tyre tread patterns are designed for different types of track surface. Large knobby treads increase traction in heavy mud or loose sand. Tight close-packed treads like these Comp 3 operate best on hard-packed surfaces.

❺ Front chain wheel spider allows the chain wheel to be changed by just loosening off these five bolts and substituting a different chain wheel to alter gearing.

❻ Chrome-moly one piece cranks. Tough, durable and suitable for older riders. Lengths vary from 170mm to 185mm. The longer they are, the more torque out the gate.

❼ Platform pedals with small studs provide a multi-directional, non-slip, footsure surface.

8 Sealed bearing or precision hubs. Keep the dirt out and stay roller smooth longer, less maintenance than unsealed hubs.

9 Front brakes are optional on the track, but essential on the street. The best are deep-jaw, side-pull calipers forged in alloy.

10 Radpads are essential for bike safety. Made of foam rubber with nylon covers, they give vital protection.

11 Gooseneck and stem clamp secures the bars to the rest of the bike. For unshiftable strength the clamp uses four bolts where ordinary bikes use only one.

12 Short, pre-bent brake lever for quick-response, one-finger action. A must for trick riding.

13 Chrome-moly, H-shape handlebars. Come in three different sizes for small, medium and big riders.

At the heart of any race-quality BMX is its frame and forks. The best are built from strong, light steels called chrome-moly and chrome-alloy. There are different grades of both. The best chrome-moly is 4130 and the top chrome-alloy is Reynolds 531. The way the tubes are joined is important. TIG welding that gives a neat stippled finish, like icing on a birthday cake, is about the strongest method.

Trick Stuff

The search for improvements in BMX machinery knows no limits. Somewhere someone is working on the most bonzai seatpost, the most radical pedal, the ultimate wheel, the super critical crank. In other words, trick stuff. These are some of the established classics.

Right: The laidback seatpost extends the distance between bars and seat. Some of the early pre-bent cro-moly laidback posts couldn't stand the strain so CW had the bright idea of including a re-inforcing bar.

Opposite: Some people like to be different..... and let the world know it. Personalising headgear is a trackside art form.

With its Concorde droopnose, aerodynamic styling, integral fibreglass seatpost and nylon seat, the Uni Seat pioneered ultra-light BMX travel, weighing in at a shade under 8 ozs.

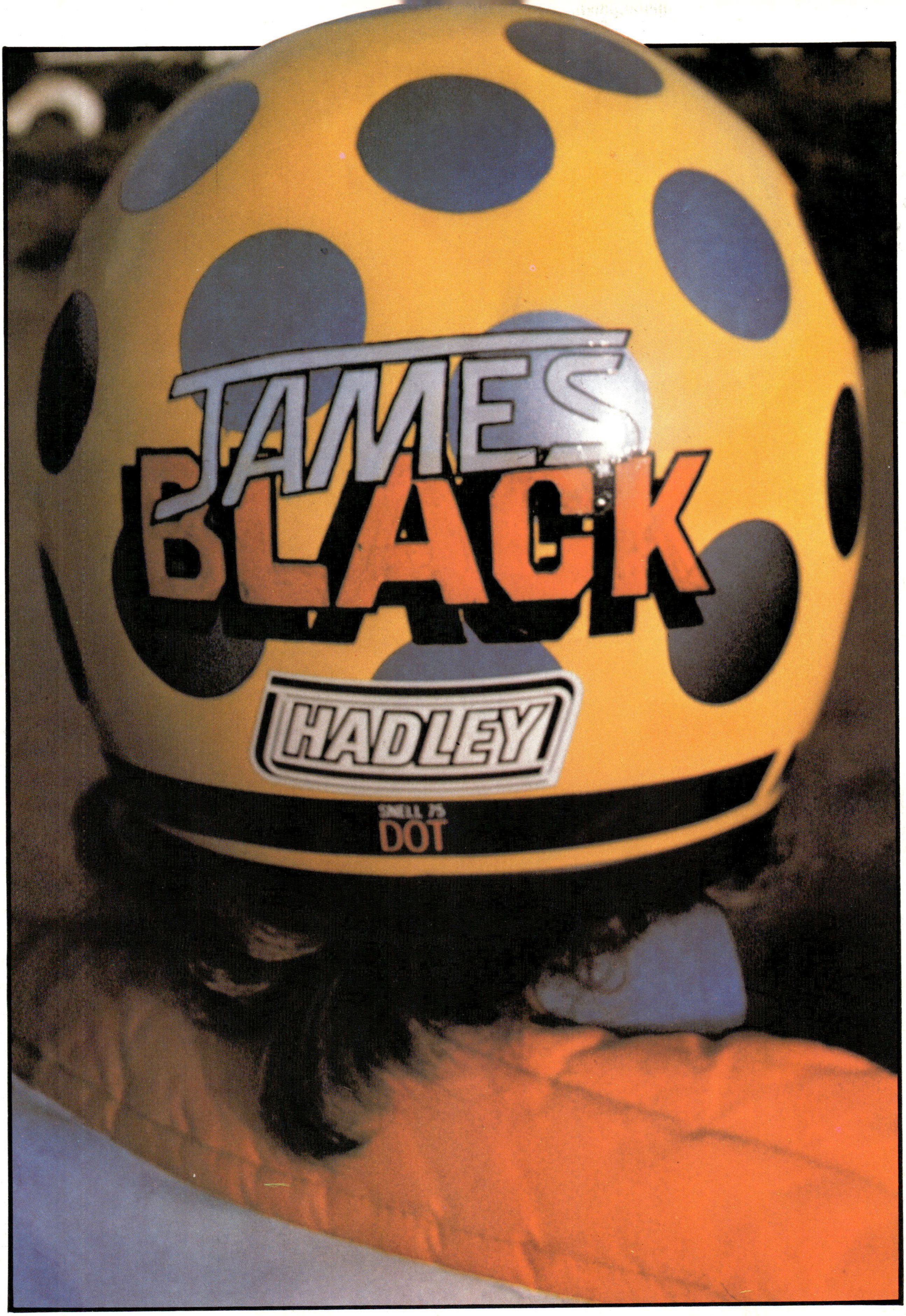
JAMES
BLACK
HADLEY
SNELL 75
DOT

Trick Stuff

Right: Radpads protect bike from rider and rider from bike. No reason why they can't match up, thought Johar, and produced chrome pads.

Below: An ounce of a revolving wheel is worth three of the frame. Mongoose proved the theory with the Pro Class wheel, with 36 holes it's 17% lighter than the rest.

Below: Oakley 3s were an instant hit. The design was inspired by grips on ski poles.

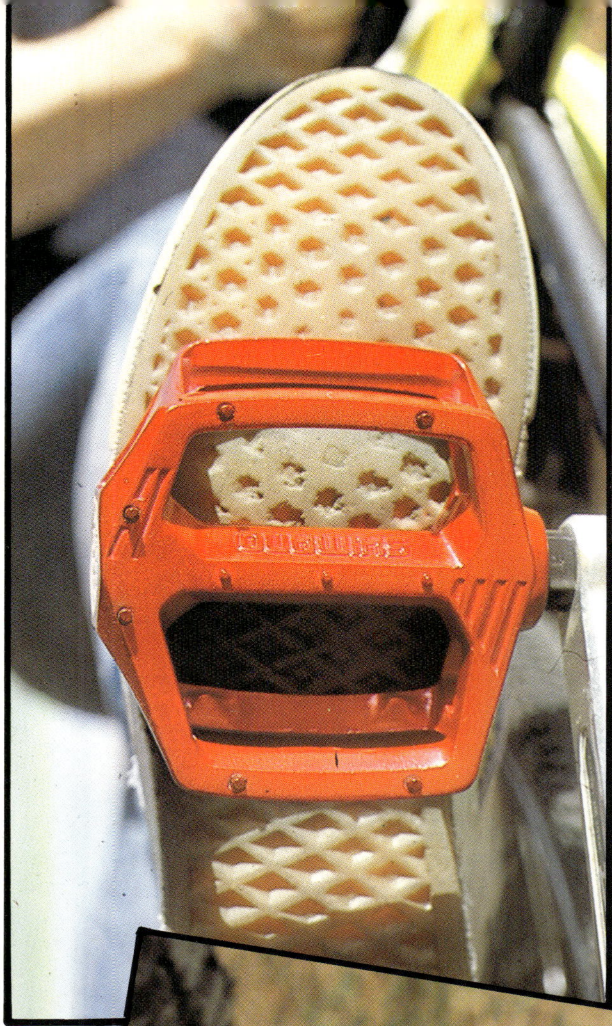

Left: Shimano's DX revolutionised pedal design. The first platform pedal, it introduced tiny studs and exploded the myth that tooth-edge cages were essential for maximum adhesion.

Below: Solid numberplates acted as windbreaks. The Aero stadium was one of the new breed of aerodynamic plates. Numbers just clip into the air holes.

Bottom of page: Small pedals and big feet didn't mix until VDC engineered these bolt-on pedal extenders. Will take up to size 15.

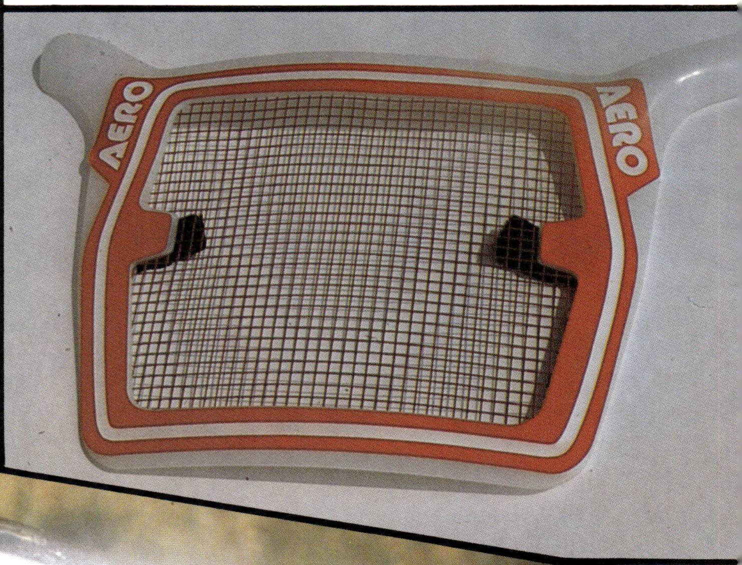

Cruisers

Slow to catch on but fast-moving in every other respect, cruisers now rate as legit BMX machinery. It wasn't always so. The first generation of the race modified beach cruisers with 26 inch rims were ace at posing but not too slick on the track. Then Joe Claveau turned up at a race with an RRS cruiser, using 24 inch wheels, and wiped out the opposition. Two inches off the rim had made all the difference. Cruisers never looked back. Today moto times are as fast as 20 inch machines.

Topline action from (top left) the World Championships. These 25-35 age group riders are twice the age of most competitors and twice as mean with it. Below left: The indoor Jag World Championships (There's more than one World Championship. Confusing, isn't it?) At both, the cruiser action is fast and furious but confined to 14s and over. An 11 year and over class is to be introduced.

More race action from the Europeans. Race technique is no different from 20 inch machines. Getting the holeshot, finding the line (and holding it) is crucial to winning. If anything, cruisers power better in the corners. The extra inch on the seat tube and the slightly taller frame makes it easier to stay feet up on the pedals as you go in tight.

Indoor Racing

When the days shorten, the nights draw in and your breath turns to ice inside your visor, then it's time to race indoors. The very first indoor BMX tracks were crude, wooden affairs on concrete floors. If you went down, it was you who took the knocks not the floors. It was more like speedway plus a few obstacles. All jumps and no berms. But as BMX grew, more promoters began staging indoor races on specially constructed dirt tracks. These are prestige events, run in large auditoriums normally used for shows, exhibitions and pop concerts. This is bright lights BMX. It comes with sound systems, spotlights, TV cameras and all the razzmatazz. The tracks are also a lot more radical, and with fewer big events in the winter months these indoor spectaculars now draw bigger crowds and higher entries.

Right: Not every indoor race is held in winter. The French organisers of the European Championships just wanted to eliminate the risk of bad weather, so they went indoors. Outside it was 33°C!

Below right: The Jag Indoor World Championships in Las Vegas, USA. The pace never let up. The track meant you had to fight for the inside lane.

Below: Birmingham's National Exhibition Centre provides the prestige indoor event in Britain's BMX calendar. The timeclock in the centre records every lap time. The best are under 25 secs. An electronic scoreboard off camera keeps spectators up to date. Two days after the race the track is flattened to make way for an equestrian event.

21
22
13
10
HARO

8

Indoor Racing

Race technique alters indoors. Tracks tend to be shorter—closer to 200 than 250 metres, and favour quick spinners. Racing is also inclined to be faster. Everyone's energy level stays higher because it's warm. It's a bit like riding on a pleasant summer's day. The body thermostat does not work overtime, like it does in winter, trying to adjust the post-race over-heating to the outside cold. The atmosphere is easier, more friendly. A bit like one big party. With grandstand seating the crowd gets a better view, and becomes more involved, more ready to shout and cheer. That gets through to the racers and, before you know it, everyone is stoked.....

Right: Indoors technique may change slightly but tactics remain the same. The first speedjump going into a right-hand berm made it an inside line track. Showing the way is Holland's Addie van der Ven.

Below right: Andy Ruffell speedjumping under close scrutiny. Was the spectator in the fourth row a talent scout or a foreign spy checking out his gooseneck?

Below: No quarter given, no quarter asked by the NEC track designer. It's easier indoors to play around with the shape of the jumps and make them gnarlier, without watching the rain wash them away.....

PL US
VITUS
24
23
16
15

Street & Bowl

The first taste for BMX action is out on the street. It's the natural place to try out a bike. First ramps are often just planks wedged tight against stacks of bricks. But those first few seconds aloft are enough to get even the smallest rider hooked. Suddenly the street is full of places to practise, paths to be bunnyhopped and kerbs to endo against.
The most fun is always undisturbed fun, so use a traffic-free area. Wear all the safety gear you can grab. Helmet. Elbow pads. Gloves. Bike pads. Now you're ready for the ultimate in concrete challenges. The Skatepark.

It's one of those twists of fate that the best skateparks were all being built just as skateboarding was on the way out. In the skateparks BMX freestyle really begins to tick. The best freestyle riders are actors, athletes, stylists and stuntmen all in one. The skateparks are their natural stage. But they don't live for an audience. Characters like Andrew Ruffell Esq, pictured here in mid-bowl aerial, can entertain himself, flipping in and out of sheer-sided bowls, swinging back and forward. A perpetual motion machine, bit by bit building up speed, rhythm and concentration. When they all come together that's the time to let it all hang out..... and then drop back in the bowl again. Other times the large key-hole shaped bowls allow enough space to gather speed and ride the vert. It's gravity-defying wall-of-death stuff to look at..... But that's not the way it feels. More like surfin' on concrete.

Find a Kerb...

Thoughtful, kind roadbuilders now provide kerbs on most new roads. This is so that BMX fanatics can spend all day practising their kerb endos! The KE is one of the simplest manoeuvres in the book (this one included). Nonetheless an endo will astonish passers-by and tell the world you've mastered the BMX handling. Until you fall off! The trick is to jam your front brake on. Pitch your weight forward and hitch the back end up just so far. Looks a cinch? Now try doing it with a friend. At the same time.

Notice the poise, the elegance of the 360, the mixed-up styling (Redline pad on a Kuwahara?) plus the thoughtful choice of setting. Now you can see how Junkyard Jim (below) earned his nickname... Lucky this book isn't in stereo!

It's not just getting up there that counts. It's also what you do when you're up there... like this front wheel cross-down. Sid looks like he's been at it all day long. Not quite. But the more height you get, the more flight you get... and the more time to freeze in mid-air for that all-important pose. Otherwise known as style.

Crash & Burn

Half the fun of BMX racing is the unexpected. The unplanned moment when nothing goes right. It can happen to the complete beginner or the seasoned pro. One moment you're out there speeding along, the next you're down in the dirt. Maybe a wheel clips a wheel, a knee and an elbow collide. Within seconds it looks chaotic. Bikes and bodies everywhere. Then as fast as it happened, it's over. Riders don't hang about to sort out who-did-what-to-whom. Finishing the race is more important. Odd cuts and bruises are the occasional scars of battle. Real injuries are few, thanks to helmets, gloves and proper protective clothing. The pain, if any, comes from hurt pride. But not every race stoppage is what it seems, as the camera can sometimes discover...

Souvenir hunters are a major track hazard. The worst belong to Grit Stuffers Anonymous. Mid-moto they drop-out of the race, sink to the floor and try to grab a keepsake of the track. This character (below) was apprehended actually putting it in his mouth.

Captured on camera (left) girls racing is more civilised than boys. Notice how the CW rider politely asks for permission to pass while Lisa executes the customary ceremonial bow before re-mounting.

Left: BMX race rules frown upon riders talking tactics with each other on track. Surprising how far some people will go to avoid being caught...

One More Time...

The meet is over. The trophies were handed out hours ago. The hot-dog seller has packed up and gone. The out-of-town team wagons have disappeared, machines on the roofracks and riders yelling goodbyes. But there's still an ounce of daylight left. Still a chance to sneak a last ride on the track. Just one more time. Just to test that drop-off. Just to tighten up the technique that will make a trophy a cert the next time. Because in BMX you know there's always going to be a next time. See ya.